A+ books

Poetry

And Then There Were Eight

Poems about Space

by Laura Purdie Salas

Capstone press

Mankato, Minnesota

The View

Earthrise
fills the skies
across the void
of space
it lies

Sky delight
blue and bright
shining in the
secret
night

3

Earth rises over the moon's horizon.

3-2-1

Waiting's over, sky is clear

Counting down now, launch is near!

Shuttle points toward deep black space

Giant step for human race

Trailing smoke clouds flaming hot —

I wish I were an astronaut!

Lost in Space

There once was a man on the moon

Who let go of his birthday balloon

"It's drifting away!"

He cried in dismay

And he looked for it all afternoon

Sky Eye

I like to look

into the sky,

a sea

of velvet black

But just last night

I realized

the sky

was looking back!

7

A nebula is a cloud of dust or gas in space.

Great Red Spot

It's not a huge red ocean

It's not a desert form

It's twice as big as Planet Earth

And it's a great red storm

It's been around three hundred years

It's still around today

According to the weatherman

This storm is here to stay

(at least until some future day

still centuries away!)

The Great Red Spot on Jupiter is actually a giant hurricane.

Moon

dances

a graceful ballet

around Earth

It decorates the

stage of sky,

shining in a spotlight of

sun

Ballerina

The Moon glows because the
Sun's light bounces off of it.

Space Walk?

Drifting

No springy step,

No ground beneath my boots —

I float throughout a black, silent

Space "walk"

12

Pluto was removed from the list of planets in 2006.

Then There Were Eight

Poor ball of ice, we know you exist; but you're

Little and solid and we must insist on

Undoing the past, so though you'll be missed, we've

Taken you

Off of the "real planet" list

Aiming High

Silver arrow to the skies, you're my mighty mirrored eyes

Finding stars and Saturn's bands, you place them gently in my hands

15

A telescope uses mirrors and light to make faraway objects appear closer.

On the Moon

No rains fall

No winds gust

A human footprint

Fixed in dust

Hours on hours

Days on days

Our magic landing

Stays and stays

17

An astronaut left this footprint on the moon in 1969.
The moon has no wind or rain to erase the footprint.

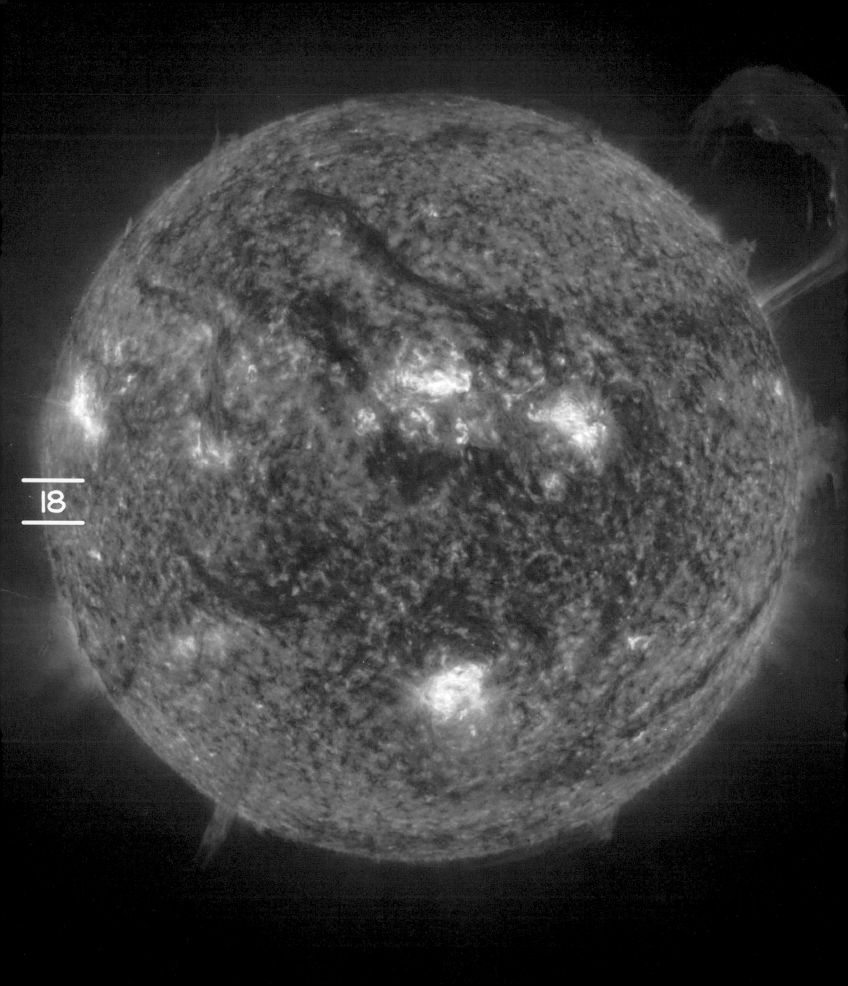

Just Right

Sun

We love you

Yes

We need you

You

Bring warmth and life and light

Come

Too close and

We

Would burn up

Go

And it's eternal night

Saturn

Saturn's

giant

Saturn's

gas

No solid

ground for

trees or grass

Saturn's

banded

Saturn

swings

A skirt of

circling

rocky rings

A Greek myth says that when a hunter chased seven sisters, Zeus changed the girls into doves. They flew to the sky and became stars.

Family Flock

Seven sisters, lovely, kind
Daughters of the sky and sea
Greedy hunter close behind
How can they stay wild and free?

Each becomes a snow-white dove
That flies up high to join the night
A brilliant flock of sister love
Soaring in forever flight

Here, Girl!

She rolls

and roams

and wags her tail

She never needs to see the vet

I love her

silver

shiny coat

She's my planetary pet!

The Mars Lander explores Mars.

26

Magic

fuschia and lime green
lights slide down night's northern sky —

winter's magic show

Energy from the sun causes northern lights to appear near the Arctic Circle.

The Language of Poetry

Couplet — two lines that end with words that rhyme

Repetition — the use of a word or phrase more than one time

Rhyme — to have an end sound that is the same as the end sound of another word

Rhythm — the pattern of beats in a poem

**Acrostic**

The subject of the poem is written straight down the page. Each line of the poem starts with a letter from the word. "Then There Were Eight" (page 13) is an acrostic poem.

Cinquain

A poem with five lines. The first line has two syllables. The second line has four, the third has six, the fourth has eight, and the last line has two syllables. "Space Walk?" (page 11) is an example of a cinquain.

Free Verse

A poem that does not follow a set pattern or rhythm. It often does not rhyme. "Ballerina" (page 10) is an example of free verse.

Haiku

A short poem that describes a scene in nature. It has five syllables in the first line, seven syllables in the second line, and five syllables in the third line. "Magic" (page 27) is an example of a haiku.

Limerick

A five-line poem that follows a certain rhythm. The first, second, and fifth lines rhyme, and so do the third and fourth lines. "Lost in Space" (page 5) is a limerick.

Glossary

astronaut (ASS-truh-nawt) — someone who travels in space

banded (BAND-id) — striped

brilliant (BRIL-yuhnt) — shining very brightly

century (SEN-chuh-ree) — a period of 100 years

dismay (diss-MAY) — worry

earthrise (URTH-rize) — the Earth appearing in the sky; an earthrise is seen from outer space.

eternal (i-TUR-nuhl) — lasting forever

fuschia (FEW-shah) — a dark purplish-red color

launch (LAWNCH) — to send a rocket up into space

void (VOID) — an empty space

Read More

Florian, Douglas. *Comets, Stars, the Moon, and Mars: Space Poems and Paintings*. Orlando, Fla.: Harcourt, 2007.

Foster, John, editor. *Space Poems*. New York: Oxford University Press, 2008.

Internet Sites

Facthound offers a safe, fun way to find Internet sites related to this book. All of the sites on FactHound have been researched by our staff.

Here's how:

1. Visit www.facthound.com

2. Choose your grade level.

3. Type in this book ID **142961207X** for age-appropriate sites. You may also browse subjects by clicking on letters, or by clicking on pictures and words.

4. Click on the **Fetch It** button.

FactHound will fetch the best sites for you!

Index of Poems

3-2-1, 4

Aiming High, 14

Ballerina, 10

Family Flock, 23

Great Red Spot, 8

Here, Girl!, 24

Just Right, 19

Lost in Space, 5

Magic, 27

On the Moon, 16

Saturn, 20

Sky Eye, 6

Space Walk?, 11

Then There Were
Eight, 13

View, The, 2

32

A+ Books are published by Capstone Press,
151 Good Counsel Drive, P.O. Box 669, Mankato, Minnesota 56002.
www.capstonepress.com

1 2 3 4 5 6 13 12 11 10 09 08

Library of Congress Cataloging-in-Publication Data
Salas, Laura Purdie.
    And then there were eight: poems about space/by Laura Purdie Salas.
    p. cm. — (A+ books. Poetry)
    Includes bibliographical references and index.
    Summary: "A collection of original, space-themed poetry for children accompanied
by striking photos. The book demonstrates a variety of common poetic forms and
defines poetic devices" — Provided by publisher.
    ISBN-13: 978-1-4296-1207-4 (hardcover)
    ISBN-10: 1-4296-1207-X (hardcover)
    ISBN-13: 978-1-4296-1747-5 (softcover)
    ISBN-10: 1-4296-1747-0 (softcover)
    1. Outer space — Juvenile poetry. 2. Children's poetry, American. I. Title. II. Series.
PS3619.A4256A53 2008
811'.6 — dc22   2007022404

Credits
Jenny Marks, editor; Ted Williams, designer; Scott Thoms, photo researcher

Photo Credits
Getty Images Inc./Stock Connection/Colin Bogucki, 26–27
iStockphoto/Lars Lentz, 20–21
NASA, 12, 16–17; JPL/ESA, 18; JPL/University of Arizona, 8–9; JPL-Caltech, 7, 25;
    JSC, 5, 10; KSC, 4
Shutterstock/Anastasiya Igolkina, cover, 1, 28; David W. Kelley, 11; Knud
    Nielsen, 15; Paul LeFevre, 22–23; Stasys Eidiejus, 2–3

Note to Parents, Teachers, and Librarians
And Then There Were Eight: Poems about Space uses colorful photographs and
a nonfiction format to introduce children to poetry and outer space themes.
This book is designed to be read independently by an early reader or to be read
aloud to a pre-reader. The images help early readers and listeners understand
the poems and concepts discussed. The book encourages further learning by
including the following sections: The Language of Poetry, Glossary, Read More,
Internet Sites, and Index. Early readers may need assistance using these features.